Heirlooms from Loving Hands

Making Memories to Cherish Forever

WRITTEN & ILLUSTRATED BY

Sandy Lynam Clough

HARVEST HOUSE PUBLISHERS

Eugene, Oregon

In cooperation with the international Christian relief organization Samaritan's Purse, a portion of the proceeds from this book will be used to buy sewing machines for women in refugee situations or developing countries and help them develop skills that will enable them to provide for themselves and their families. For more information please write: Samaritan's Purse, P.O. Box 3000, Boone, NC 28607.

Heirlooms from Loving Hands

Sandy Clough Studios
25 Trail Road
Marietta, GA 30064
1-800-447-8409

Design and Production by Garborg Design Works, Minneapolis, Minnesota

Scripture quotations are from Scripture quotations are from the King James Version; the Holy Bible, New International®. Copyright ©1973, 1978, 1984 by the International Bible Society. Used by permission of Zondervan Publishing House; The Living Bible, Copyright © 1971 owned by assignment by Illinois Regional Bank N.A. (as trustee). Used by permission of Tyndale House Publishers, Inc., Wheaton, Illinois 60189. All rights reserved.

Clough, Sandy Lynam, 1948-
    Heirlooms from loving hands / Sandy Lynam Clough.
        p.   cm.
    ISBN 1-56507-609-5
    1. Needlework.   2. Needlework--History.   3. Heirlooms.   I. Title.
TT750.C58 1998
746.4--dc21   97-46938
                                                          CIP

DEDICATION

To my parents, Susie and Myron Lynam, who have
provided so many opportunities for me to explore
and develop the gift of creativity.

To my husband, Rick, who makes it possible for me
to do everything that I do.

And to my sons, Samuel and Jeremy, who have
delighted me with their own creativity.

SPECIAL THANKS

To Vickie Scheider, for the generous and
continuous use of her antiques in my paintings.

A Heritage of Joy

As my pen is poised over the pages of my black spiral-bound notebook, I try to paint my thoughts with words that will put windows to my memories and my heart. Sometimes the perfect words come in just the right sentence structure (usually when I'm in the bathtub!), and I wonder if I really could be a writer. But at other times it seems that all the words I have ever known just packed their bags and left town! Then I remember that I am not a writer by trade. I am an artist. It is my life's work to reveal my heart with brush and paint.

But I wrote this book to tell you some of my stories and to share with you a special joy in my life—the joy of inspiration, the joy of heart and hand working together in a sometimes-sacrificial labor of love, the joy of creating, the joy that comes with sharing those efforts, and the joy that people receive from our gift. I have found this joy in work done with needle and thread, but that is only one of many paths of creativity. If you don't yet know this joy, my story is for you so that you will taste the pleasure and perhaps try your hand at creating. If you have already experienced this joy, you will recognize it immediately in the stories I tell. My story will be your story, and you'll sense that our hearts are connected by the same thread of creativity and joy that has connected loving hands for generations.

Hands

Hands that throw kisses
Hands that smooth hair
Hands that cook supper
And then fold in prayer.

Hands that wave bye-bye
Hands that wipe tears
Hands that keep busy
And hands that calm fears.

Hands that plant gardens
Hands that sweep floors
Hands that tie ribbons
And do so much more.

Hands must wash dishes
Hands must make beds.
But hands still find time
For needles and thread.

Crochet and quilting,
Embroidery, too—
Such beautiful skills
These hands find to do.

They work with a joy
That we all understand
And leave us keepsakes and heirlooms
From these loving hands.

Sandy Lynam Clough

Sandy Lynam Clough

A Common Thread

Just as the knot at the end of a thread anchors it in a piece of needlework, an individual person can anchor the joy of creativity that becomes part of a family's heritage. Perhaps some of your family ties are made with needle and thread. Did your grandmother pass on a tradition of creative hands? Did you have a special aunt who shared her skills and creativity? Or you might be the pioneer of a creative lifestyle and tradition in your family. I want to tell you about a young woman who lived in the early 1900s. I see in her the joyful thread of creativity that runs through my family even today.

Even when she was only a teenager, this young woman was a very accomplished seamstress. She had learned her skills from her mother, and people would invite this talented woman to their homes to make fine garments for them. She would stay in each home until she had made all the clothes they needed, including the beautiful dresses with the rows of lace, fine details, and fancy trims so popular at that time. When she finished her work, she would drive her horse and buggy to another home and sew for that family.

This young woman married a farmer who was a widower with four children. They lived in a simple farmhouse. It had four large rooms, with a large porch across the front for rocking chairs, a swing, and, in the summer, lovely plants. The house had a tin roof and a well on the back porch with a red-and-white dipper and bucket. It didn't have indoor plumbing or electricity. And in this house she gave birth to eleven children.

As a mother to fourteen children (she lost one to pneumonia), she worked hard to maintain her household. She cooked meals, canned food, scrubbed stacks of dishes, washed clothes, and made all the linens and clothing her family needed. She made bibs and diapers for the babies and sheets and pillowcases for the beds. She used her skills to provide for every member of her household.

The days started early on the farm, and at night they had only oil lamps to see by. But when her work was done, or she had a quiet moment, or she was holding or nursing a baby, she would crochet beautiful doilies, bedspreads, and tablecloths or embroider on household items she had already made. She used her needle to add a touch of beauty to pillowcases, children's collars, and baby dresses.

This diligent woman was my grandmother, and when I heard the story of her early years from my mother for the first time, I saw a common thread running through our family from generation to generation. I'd never noticed this thread of joy before, but it may run through your family. I invite you to take a look.

The Joy of Creating

Why would a woman with fourteen children be willing to do anything except what needed to be done to manage a home and care for her family? Where did she find the time and energy to embroider and why would she want to crochet? I asked my mother if Grandma did her needlework to make gifts for her friends. But my mother explained that she didn't do it for gifts because her friends did the same kinds of needlework themselves.

Why did Grandma do her needlework? I know why she did it! I understand because ever since I was a little girl, I've known the joy of making something with my own hands—whether it was a doll dress or the veil to my wedding gown. Grandma did her needlework for the joy of creating, for the satisfaction of making something beautiful with her hands. Her heart motivated her hands, and those loving hands beautified even everyday things. A lacy crocheted tablecloth made an ordinary table something special, and a colorful quilt added character and charm to her home. These touches of beauty were not expensive except in the time and care she spent on them. I'm sure her needlework was not at all a chore because of the joy she experienced as she made something beautiful.

Think about the duties and tasks of your day-to-day world. As you do them, which ones give you an opportunity to make your world a little more beautiful? Perhaps folding the dinner napkins in a special way, bringing into your house some flowers or even a single stem from the garden, or adding a colorful sticker to letters you mail—little acts like these add touches of beauty to one's life.

I only have two of those doilies that my grandmother crocheted. Although it means a great deal to me just to have them, thinking about how she must have enjoyed creating them truly makes them heirlooms from loving hands.

Something Nobody Undid

As an artist and also a mother of young children, I used to say that painting was the only thing I did that nobody undid. I'm sure you know that feeling. When I cooked food, my family ate it. When I washed the clothes, they wore them. When I cleaned the house, they got it dirty. But my paintings have lasted. It seemed that my paintings were all I had to show for my efforts because nobody undid them!

Perhaps the handmade heirlooms and keepsakes that we so treasure—whether a handkerchief with tatting on the edge, a needlepoint pillow, a smocked baby dress, a hand-knit scarf, or an embroidered tea towel—were also the things someone did that nobody else undid.

This kind of work that wasn't undone gives us keepsakes that are tangible reminders of loving hands. Oh, they don't tell us all the things that loving hands do. After all, loving hands cook meals, wash dishes, and do laundry. They also bandage skinned knees and wipe away tears. But these handmade keepsakes give us something tangible to hold even when we forget the other things that loving hands do. Those acts of love that we depend on and take for granted fade into our memories, but these treasures give us something to touch. When we can hold something that was handmade by someone we love, we really do have an heirloom from loving hands.

The Heart Behind the Hands

Sometimes I'll see advertised in a magazine a product described as "heirloom quality." That phrase may mean that the product is made so well that it would last for generations. But that's not what "heirloom quality" means to me. Instead, an heirloom is something made by somebody I love. The person who created the object makes that object a treasure. The heart behind the hands—the labor of love—makes it an item to love.

Today we can buy a lot of things that people used to make by hand at home. Department and home-decorating stores offer beautifully-patterned quilts, and imported doilies hang on racks for us to purchase. You can buy lovely crocheted tablecloths and bedspreads. Needlepoint pillows and embroidered linens, place mats, and napkins are available to give our homes a beautiful heirloom look. We like the look, and we buy these pretty things because most of us don't have as many heirlooms as we would like. But I don't think for a moment any of us consider the items we purchase to be heirlooms. How could they be heirlooms when we don't know the people who made them?

11

In fact, when we have things that have been made by someone we love, I don't think the quality even matters. A treasured dresser scarf may be frayed or faded; it might even have a hole worn in it. But if it was made by someone we love, we really don't care. So I pass right by all those beautiful quilts in the store. The one I treasure isn't even finished. My grandmother started it, and it's just pieced from plain squares out of the scrap bag—one or two pieces from the fabric used to make a dress or skirt for me. That is the quilt I want to save. It's made by someone I love.

So keeping in mind that an heirloom is something made by someone you love, look around your home. What heirlooms do you have—or what heirlooms have you made for others?

LINKS TO THE PAST

In the Victorian era a favorite sentiment was "Remember me." Those simple words are found on Victorian teacups, calling cards, and samplers that were hung on the wall. Sometimes I think that is the heart cry of all of us—"Remember me"—as we become separated from friends and family by time and distance.

I thank my God upon
every remembrance of you.

THE BOOK OF PHILIPPIANS

Yesterday's Seamstress

When I was growing up, I thought my mother could make anything—because she could! She knew how to make draperies, our clothing, tablecloths, aprons, and even bedspreads. It seemed that she had always known how to sew, but she actually learned to sew as a young girl with her mother, just as I did. My mother learned to sew at about the time she started school. She learned by sitting on her mother's lap at the Singer treadle sewing machine that had been paid for with eggs. (Grandma got five cents credit for each dozen eggs.)

As she learned to sew, my mother worked with my grandmother making clothes and linens for their large family. But not all of the fabric for their sewing was purchased from a store. "Short sacks"—those 100-pound feed sacks used on the farm—provided a plain white fabric that could be used for pillowcases, sheets, dish towels, and tablecloths. They could wash the sacks with lye to make the fabric whiter. Flour sacks were sometimes a print fabric, and my grandmother and mother made bloomers, skirts, slips, and dresses out of them. When store-bought fabric was affordable, they made their sheets, pillowcases, and curtains out of white or yellow "domestic cloth." When my grandfather sold a bale of cotton, they would buy bolts of blue chambray and cotton print. The print fabric was for the girls, and the blue chambray would become shirts for the boys to wear with their overalls. They made bibs for the babies out of flour sacks, and my grandmother taught my mother how to embroider on those. Sometimes they copied designs out of a Sears Roebuck catalog. My grandmother also added tatting to the edge of the pillowcases.

Sandy Lynam Clough

They didn't buy dress patterns, but my grandmother was such a good seamstress that she made her own patterns from pages of used calendars or old catalogs. She would pin the pages together, hold them up against the person she was sewing for, and adjust her pattern to make it fit.

That treadle sewing machine—paid for with eggs—sits in my home today. Although it was a work horse of a machine for a big family, loving hands made it an instrument of joy. As you use your creative hands to show love to others, the tools you use—as well as what you make with them—may someday be a treasure. The crochet hook you use to make afghans for a nursing home, the pen you use to write an encouraging thought to a friend in calligraphy, or the special tools you use to beautifully decorate cakes are instruments of joy for the one who gives and the one who receives.

THE SINGER SEWING MACHINE

Isaac M. Singer wasn't the first to develop a sewing machine. In the 1840s, Walter Hunt designed a machine using an eye-point needle and a threaded shuttle. But he abandoned the project out of concern that his invention would leave poor seamstresses without work.

In 1850, Isaac Singer produced the first truly practical machine for sewing. It had an overhanging arm, a table for supporting the material, a presser foot to hold the fabric down, a feed wheel to move the fabric under the needle, and—the real breakthrough—a foot pedal instead of a hand crank. The sewer could now have both hands free to maneuver the cloth as it moved under the needle.

Singer didn't stop with inventing. He also pioneered installment buying and a system for providing service along with sales—and he was the first to introduce the idea of trade-ins so that even the less wealthy could own a Singer.

A Thread of Joy

Mama says there was never enough spare time or enough fabric for her to sew as much as she wanted to when she was growing up. She had chores to do. Every morning and every evening she had 37 cows to milk. She also helped her mother cook biscuits for break-fast, and of course she went to school. She helped hoe corn and cotton in the fields as well.

When I asked Mama why she liked to sew so much, she looked at me, kind of tucked her chin, and grinned a little—and I knew. There it was again—that thread of joy. She told me it was fun to cut out the fabric and watch the project come together.

Mama could have viewed her sewing as one more item on her to-do list, but instead she found in it the joy that comes with being creative. What a wonderful encouragement for each of us!

You can create new heirlooms,
and the memories that make them special,
just by owning them.

ELAINE MARKOUTSAS

CLOTHES FOR A LIFETIME

When I was a teenager, I had sewing lessons from the Singer store downtown and in my home economics classes at school, but it was really my mama who taught me how to sew and wove this thread of joy throughout my life. Mama sewed my clothes from the time I was a baby, and together we made my wedding dress. When I look back through old photos, I see her handiwork on me. I see a toddler with a pink organdy dress with little flowers embroidered in French knots on the yoke. There's a red organdy ruffled dress for my first birthday party. I see new dotted Swiss for summer, navy taffeta for Sunday, and velveteen for Christmas. The years go by with cotton plaids for back-to-school and wool skirts for winter. Every year is punctuated by a new Easter dress. The high-school years called for Madras plaid and a red taffeta Scarlett O'Hara costume. After pageant clothes and miniskirts for my college years, my mama made me a lovely wedding dress. I helped trim the lace, glued on the pearls, and made the veil and train.

When I think of all she made, I don't know where she found the time. My mother was always busy. I still wish I had her energy. She worked fast, and she had her shortcuts. (Patterns weren't pinned to the fabric to be cut out. They were held down by silverware. Knives did the best job because they were heavy and flat.) It seemed to me that the only times Mama was still for very long was when she was fishing or sewing!

SEWING ROOM TREASURES

When Mama was at the sewing machine, I liked to be in the room even when the whrrrr of the machine prevented conversation. In between fittings, I could go through the button jar (our family history in a jar!) and look for buttons. To avoid a trip to the store, it was usually my mission to find enough small white buttons for a blouse or a button for the waistband on a skirt.

I would scoop up the buttons in my hands and let them ripple through my fingers. There were glass buttons and pearl buttons, gold buttons and silver buttons. There were shirt buttons and blazer buttons, covered buttons and rhinestone buttons. My favorite were the tiny baby buttons. Among a brown button from my daddy's khaki work shirt, a lovely rhinestone-and-pearl button from Mama's dressy pink blouse, and a button from a winter car coat, I was sure to find nautical buttons. ("Sailor" fashion was a favorite theme for our sewing in the spring.) There always seemed to be an amazing variety of small white buttons that didn't match each other.

Interspersed with this most personal collection were brand new buttons that, for some reason, had never been used. They were pretty, shiny, and bright (and sometimes still on their cards), but they had no stories to tell, for they had never gone with us to the first day of school or to church or even to the lake fishing.

It was so much fun to pour the buttons out onto the bedspread. I never realized how many buttons—and memories—there were until I had to pick each one up and put it back in the jar!

The Fellowship of Creativity

When Mama had sewn enough for me to try on her latest creation, I gingerly stepped into the skirt, carefully pulled on the top, and—ouch!—usually found a pin. As I got older, the final fitting was often a battle of the wills. I wanted the hemline higher and higher, and Mama wanted it lower and lower. We eventually bargained our way to a compromise.

Every afternoon spent sewing was interrupted by what Mama called a "tea party." We never really poured tea, but we took a break and had a little snack together. Mama had her coffee and I had a Coke.

When Mama went back to sewing, I could go through her old suitcase of dress patterns and dream. When a dress we couldn't afford was advertised in the newspaper, we could pull a sleeve pattern out of one envelope, a bodice from another, a certain collar from a third, and construct the dress I wanted. This kind of creativity helped me have what I dreamed about! The joy of creativity can indeed make dreams come true for all of us!

THE KINSHIP OF CREATIVITY

There are some outfits I choose today that make me think, Mama would like this, and I know she would be pleased with my choice. It recently occurred to me that it isn't coincidental that I happen to choose clothes that she likes. Actually, I choose them because she likes them. My ideas of good taste and style as well as my knowledge of fabric came from being near Mama as she sewed. I know that the appeal I find in navy and white outfits for spring is no accident. I also learned from her about the nap in certain fabrics and how to iron on the wrong side. I learned what fabrics would wear well and which ones would look cheap.

At her old Singer sewing machine, Mama taught me how to sew— but she taught me so much more. Those hours together unleashed in me a creativity with fabric and thread and gave me the confidence that I could make what I wanted.

What skill could you share with someone the way my mama shared her sewing with me? Or what someone in your life could share a skill with you? Make the arrange- ments to get together to cook or do needlework or stencil or practice calligraphy or quilt or work on a photo album....The list goes on and on! You'll find that there's something unique and very special about the kinship of creativity!

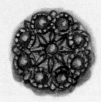

SIMPLE SEWING IDEAS

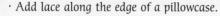

- Add lace along the edge of a pillowcase.
- Discover the ease and fun of StitchWitchery® at your local fabric shop and iron fabrics together instead of sewing!
- Pick up a glue gun at the local hardware store and, again, skip the needle and thread!
- You might enjoy the whimsy of a little table-top sewing tree. Spools of thread, small scissors, and large buttons could hang as ornaments, and a tape measure could be draped as a garland.
- Decorate your sewing spot with a "sewing wreath." Attach vintage sewing notions like old cards of buttons as well as antique thimbles or scissors to a grapevine wreath or a wreath of dried flowers.

OCCASIONS TO SEW

- Welcome a family's newest addition with a sampler, a bib, or a simple blanket.
- Personalize a pair of pillowcases with "Mr. & Mrs." or a pair of towels with "His" and "Hers" for the bride and groom.
- Make a memory by sewing a costume for a school play or dress-up fun at home.
- A simple Christmas ornament (crocheted, glued, bejeweled, sewn) will bring special joy each year.
- Celebrate Easter with a special tablecloth and napkins that you bring out on that joyous spring day.
- What Fourth of July table wouldn't be more festive with red-white-and-blue napkins that you can use every year?
- Start a family tradition with special table linens for every birthday you celebrate. You might even sew a "Happy Birthday!" banner to hang on those special days!

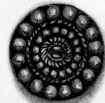

Lessons from the Sewing Room

Not all of my clothes were homemade, but I don't think shopping for clothes ever involves the same kind of anticipation that sewing does. When I go shopping, I don't know whether or not I will find anything I like. But how many times have I heard someone say, "If I can't find what I want, I'll just have to make it!"

When Mama and I walked into a fabric store and opened the pattern book, it became a book of possibilities. Our imaginations paired the favorite fabric with the perfect style. When the yardage was cut and the thread color matched, imagination gave way to anticipation. Soon I would have a pretty new dress!

In fact, my interest in sewing was highly motivated by my desire to have more and more pretty clothes. But in the process of learning to sew, I learned some valuable life lessons from my mama and that sewing machine. I learned to follow instructions. I learned to complete a task step-by-step in order to have what I wanted. I learned that it's easier to do something right the first time than it is to rip it out and do it over. And I learned that if I made a mistake, I had to correct it before I could move on. The thread of joy that, for me, comes with sewing came with some valuable lessons for life.

A BRIEF POSTSCRIPT

Mama quit sewing two or three years ago. She gave me her sewing cabinet filled with her thread, tape measure, scissors, thimbles, and notions. But guess what! Shortly after her 80th birthday, Mama bought herself a new sewing machine—and one for me! The joy goes on!

23

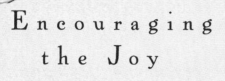

Encouraging
the Joy

It was the joy of creativity and my eagerness to
work on clothes for my doll that inspired me to take my sewing to school
when I was in first grade. But pure fear eclipsed all those warm emotions when
my teacher approached my desk and saw my little metal recipe box open and my
sewing project inside. When, holding my sewing box, she led me from the room, I had a
feeling we were headed for the principal's office. But we passed his office and turned
down the hall to another teacher's room where my teacher shared my sewing with her
co-worker as a delightful discovery. My teacher could have scolded me and ruined my
whole day, but instead she made a little six-year-old girl feel that what she was doing
was something pretty special. How wise she was to encourage the joy—and how wise you
and I are when we do the same!

A wise teacher makes learning a joy.

THE BOOK OF PROVERBS

DRESSING MY DOLLS

As a child, I didn't have many store-bought, ready-made dresses, and my dolls had only one each—the one they came in. It was my responsibility to clothe my dolls and to make sure that their clothes were appropriate for all the pretend occasions in their make-believe lives.

One of the great things about having a mother who sewed was the scrap bag. Scrounging in a sewing cabinet drawer might even turn up a partial package of sequins or beads left over from a costume or Christmas decorations. These materials could be fuel for the imagination of a young fashion designer crafting an evening gown for her doll or a costume for herself on a lazy summer afternoon.

Once, when I got interested in knitting, I even tried to knit a sweater for my doll. My mother taught me how to knit row after row, but neither one of us knew how to knit a sleeve into or onto a sweater, so I simply taped the sleeves of the blue yarn sweater in with bright red tape. If my doll was embarrassed, she never mentioned it!

In fact, even if the stitches were clumsy and the fabric had raw edges, none of my dolls ever complained about how I dressed them. Even if the dress were held together in the back with pins, they wore what I made them with grace.

MAKING TIME TO MAKE A MEMORY

Tucked away in an old camel-backed trunk in my studio is the chubby-cheeked, blonde doll that survived my childhood. She's old enough to have heirloom status, but she doesn't look at all like the beautiful "heirloom" dolls advertised in magazines, those dolls with their perfect porcelain faces and velvet dresses trimmed in lace. Part of my doll's hair is still pinned with a bobby pin, and long ago a certain little girl defined her eyebrows for her with a lead pencil. My doll doesn't have any socks or shoes on, and after all these years the elastic in her little under-wear is shot. But this doll is a treasure to me because she shared my childhood. Other people may cherish a wagon, a stuffed animal, a dress, or something else that reminds them of their child-hood, of a special time or a special place. For me, that doll brings to mind so many memories, so many stories, and so many smiles.

I don't remember the last time I played with this doll, but she is still dressed the way she was the day I put her down. She's wearing a homemade dress of a little blue rosebud print fabric. It's not one of my creations, but a doll dress my mother made. I don't know how my mother found time to make that little dress with a collar and a little pocket edged with a sweet blue embroi-dered trim. I don't even remember if I asked her to do it.

But I do remember my own little preschooler asking me over and over again to make a new outfit for his teddy bear. I had so much to do! I had two little ones to take care of and paintings to paint and housework to finish! One day I finally made time to sew something for Samuel, and he was so happy that I really regretted that I had made him wait so long. I'm so glad now that I finally took time to make that memory. Little boys (and girls) grow up quickly, and that turned out to be my only opportunity to dress one of his toys.

Children ask their mothers to make many different things for them—doll dresses, Superman capes, paper crowns, or angel wings. Although few of these survive childhood and achieve heir-loom status, a mother who takes time to make *anything* for her child creates for him a lasting memory of her loving hands and attentive heart.

Loving Legacy of Lace

It's easy to have a love affair with lace. The very word is synonymous with romance!

It may surprise you to learn that, in the 1800s, many women made intricate laces at home. A lace like Battenburg was made by placing or pinning the lace braid along the design that had been stamped on heavy paper. (The design, as well as the lace braid, were purchased.) The needleworker then followed the fine lines with needle and thread using a chain stitch or other lace stitch to fill in the design between the braids. Crocheted lace was made using linen or cotton thread and a crochet hook. Antique Point lace includes such stitches as Brussels lace, Venetian lace, English lace, and Spanish lace. All of these could be learned and worked into absolutely exquisite lace using fine threads.

I have to admit that I've never considered trying to make lace at home. But I know a woman who does just that. Betty Kemp is keeping the 500-year-old art of bobbin lace alive. She has done crocheting and knitting since childhood, but this 74-year-old needleworker didn't learn lacemaking until she was in her forties.

Mrs. Kemp begins the process by winding her thread (linen and cotton work best, but all kinds of thread can be used) onto a bobbin. Then, using a pattern she places on a pillow, she sticks straight pins in the appropriate spots and weaves the threads around them. Using just two stitches (the cloth or whole stitch and the half-stitch), she weaves lace garters, wall hangings, crosses, bookmarks, handkerchief edgings, table mats, and flowers.

Her lace creations take a lot of time and patience, but she doesn't sell them when she's done. Instead, she gives them away to relatives, friends, and even strangers. "It's the biggest volunteer thing I do," Mrs. Kemp says. As she demonstrates her art, teaches her skill to others, and gives away the fruit of her labors, her loving hands are spreading joy.

Quilted Comfort for the Heart

Long before any of us thought of quilts as antiques or keepsakes, they were simply part of our lives. We used them to keep warm in bed, spread them on the grass for Baby to play on, threw them on the sand for a picnic at the beach, and wrapped furniture in them when we moved. The people who made quilts might be amused to see how we treasure them. Their quilts were part of the living that happened in our parents' and grandparents' homes, but we hang them on walls as works of art, we drape them on accent tables, and we decorate bedrooms around them.

But these quilts we prize and often pamper were necessities of life. After all, the houses of yesterday were heated by fireplaces, so at night when the fires died down and the bedrooms got very cold, those quilts—those layers of warmth stitched together with love and skill—were very important. They also offered comfort for the heart and beauty for the eye.

28

FRUGAL AND FUN, DELICATE AND DURABLE

Why would someone take time to piece together many little pieces to make a quilt? Why didn't our grandmothers and great-grandmothers simply gather several yards of fabric, use it to sandwich some cotton batting, tack the layers together, and be done? Well, putting together all those little pieces allowed the quilter to use fabric scraps from clothing or other sewing projects, scraps that would otherwise be wasted. Piecing quilts was a frugal way to provide warmth for the family.

And piecing quilts became an art in itself. Even when the fabric choices were limited, the artistic creativity of many homemakers shines through in the quilts that have survived. Some quilters simply pieced together squares while others followed patterns that we now regard as traditional. These decorative patterns were given such imaginative names as "Step Around the Mountain" and "Flying Geese." Then there were the "crazy quilts" made from oddly-shaped scraps, including satin and velvet. Decorative embroidery covered the seams between the pieces of crazy quilts, and it wasn't uncommon to find a flower stitched in the middle of a piece. Appliquéd quilts featured designs cut out of colorful fabric and appliquéd to a plain square with decorative stitches. "Dresden Plate," "Sunbonnet Sue," and "Overall Sam" were popular designs for appliquéd quilts, and many of us grew up with Sunbonnet Sue and Overall Sam. I wish I had a pattern for every version of these two characters. It would be a charming collection.

Most of us do remember quilts, but do we think often enough of the tiny stitches that hold these quilts together—and the hands that put them there? Do we think of Mama sitting at her mama's feet while the womenfolk did the quilting and the chatting? Sometimes the stitches were done in businesslike straight rows, but other times the stitches formed an intricate design. In either case, these delicate but durable quilting stitches came from hands that took pride in doing their work very well and very carefully.

SHARING THE QUILTING JOY

Although making a quilt can be a solitary project, many have been finished at quilting bees where women came together in a labor of love to work and to enjoy each other's company. At these quilting bees, the quilt was often stretched on a frame, and the ladies would sit around it doing those tiny stitches that hold the quilt together. It was a big job, but—as the Amish say—"Many hands make light work."

Those many hands also made for community. As women gathered with their needle and thread, they shared the concerns of their hearts, the joys of life, the challenges of the day-to-day, and their dreams for the future. Clearly, the quilt was not the only important end result! Relationships were built, friendships were crafted, hearts were encouraged, and spirits were warmed.

My grandmother hosted many quilting bees in her home. When I asked my mother whether grandmother and her friends took turns going to each other's homes, she said, "No, they always came to our house." So, I asked her, "did they take turns keeping the finished quilt?" She said, "No, we always got the quilts because there were so many of us."

The ladies went to my grandmother's house every week to quilt. (My aunt tells me that, as a little girl, she liked to eavesdrop and hear the latest gossip she wasn't supposed to hear!) At one of those quilting bees, when my grandmother wasn't feeling well, my mother first learned to sew. Apparently she had gotten underfoot, so one of the women gave her a needle and thread and taught her the briar stitch. Mama was only four years old, but that was old enough to pick up the thread of joy.

Sandy Lynam Clough

Tools of Loving Hands

Just as we cherish the needlework made by loving hands, the tools and notions that those loving hands used can also invoke sweet memories....

I'm sitting in front of my grandmother's old Singer treadle sewing machine. The head is richly decorated with a gold design. The metal on the end has a beautiful design of trailing leaves and vines stamped in it. It almost looks engraved. The machine itself is set in a dark wood cabinet with two pairs of drawers. This old Singer is definitely antique, but it's no museum piece. It bears the scars not from abuse, but from use. The wood veneer has chips in it, and part of the gold design has been worn off by the yard after yard of fabric that slid across it. But that's why this old sewing machine, paid for with eggs, is so beautiful to me. It's beautiful because my grandmother used it. If it were perfect, I suppose it would be an inheritance, but instead it's my heritage, a heritage of working and creating with my hands. I can pass that machine—and other things I treasure—on through my children to the next generation and, I hope, on to the next.

When I started this book, Mama gave me my grandmother's thimble. I've seen beautifully engraved sterling silver thimbles in antique stores, but I've never seen a thimble quite like this one. It was used so much that it is even split on the edge and misshapen. It may even have been stepped on or rocked on a time or two!

I also have the sewing machine my mama used as I grew up. Some of the clothes made on it blur in my mind, but my memories of her sewing are memories of that machine.

Many items can remind us of the sewing and needlework of yesteryear. You may want to collect only family items; you might choose one particular item, like a thimble, that has a special meaning for you; or you may want to try to get a variety of these vintage tools before they disappear. Whatever you decide, enjoy looking for old sewing baskets, dress forms, vintage patterns, pin cushions, darning eggs, scissors, tape measures, embroidery hoops, knitting needles, wooden spools of thread, and old buttons.

Whatever you collect—sewing tools or the needlework itself—think of yourself as a steward, not merely an owner. You have an opportunity not only to own these things but also to care for them and pass them on. After all, you are carrying a thread of knowledge into another generation as you display some of the pieces that were made or some of the tools involved in the making. And when you share what you have learned, don't forget to mention the joy!

B U T T O N ,   B U T T O N . . .

If you have a collection of vintage buttons...

· Sew several buttons onto a favorite blouse. Choose a different button for every buttonhole.

· Decorate a vest to show off some of your favorites!

· Make earrings out of antique buttons by using a glue gun to mount them on earring parts available at craft stores.

CLEAN AND PURE

Sandy Lynam Clough

Words from Times Past

For generations women have affected the values and character of their families with sewing and needlework. It seems to me that part of our culture has literally been carried on a needle—gliding in and out of our lives, pulling a thread of beauty as well as duty. By turning a chore into a grace, women have exemplified patient diligence, the satisfaction of accomplishment, and the joy of creating.

In the past, when the virtues of faith, hope, and love were woven into the fabric of life, women declared these virtues in the needlework they did for their families. These messages were often words to live by. On pillows, wall-hangings, bed linens, tea towels, and doilies, they stitched lovely flowers and messages such as "Kindness Makes Friends" and "God Bless Our Home." My friend Vickie has a set of antique pillowcases embroidered with "I slept and dreamt that life was beauty, I awoke and found that life was duty." Tea towels were embroidered with the days of the week. Mothers would embroider "Mr. & Mrs." on pillowcases for their soon-to-be-married daughters. And a favorite sentiment in the Victorian era was "Remember me," a phrase so endearing we all long to see it.

A FEW WORDS

When I go antiquing, I'm always drawn to these framed mottoes, many of which are stitched on punched paper rather than fabric. I look for mottoes because so many of them touch my heart. They say things I want my walls to say like "Welcome" or "Rock of Ages, Cleft for Me," things that will help people who visit our home know us a little better. Whether we display our sense of humor or hang our hearts on the wall, our homes are more personal when we share our thoughts. I once visited in the home of a dear lady who had hanging over the kitchen sink the simple prayer "Lord, make me like an old blue blanket." I knew immediately there was no pretension in her home, only a desire to make people feel welcome and comfortable.

Today counted cross-stitch is probably the most popular way to stitch a motto, and a wide selection is available on charts. If you can't find the one you want, simply purchase a chart of an alphabet style you like and chart your own message.

But when you come across a framed motto or a message stitched on linens, don't forget the reason why so many of these treasures are around. Someone took the time to stitch them. When we handle these hand-sewn items that are yellow or soft with age, we may find ourselves in awe because they were made with the most precious commodity in our economy today—time.

A FEW LETTERS

Embroidered monograms make household linens personal and elegant. Today's sewing machines can not only stitch monograms, but they can also embroider. This option makes it possible for a busy woman to decorate her linens in a distinctive way even if she doesn't have time for handwork. Monogrammed linens are also thoughtful gifts. Everyone likes to see their name (or initials) in print!

Monogramming has its roots back in the Middle Ages when families identified their precious few linens with their coat of arms or another unique mark. Royalty also embroidered their linens, but in the 19th century, the rising bourgeoisie asserted themselves and followed that lead.

Monogramming also became a way of preserving a family's maternal name.

Beginning at an early age, a young girl would monogram linens for her hope chest. Later she would receive wedding gifts with entwined initials.

From World War I until the 1950s, department stores hired women to carry on this tradition and provide monogrammed linens for their customers.

Big Hands

*A good man leaves an inheritance
for his children's children.*

THE BOOK OF PROVERBS

I think I've always known that big hands do things that make my life easier and, at the same time, leave special memories....

Big hands hold storybooks and the funny paper; big hands pick up garden snakes and bait fish hooks. Big hands dig deep into pockets for nickels for the ice cream truck, and big hands play ball. Big hands make cars run, and big hands plant gardens.

These tangible things that big hands make connect us in a special way to those big hearts. These heirlooms from loving hands speak unspoken feelings of love and call to mind their owner's dependability and resourcefulness. And in the craftsmanship of these heirlooms, the satisfaction of creating shines through.

There is no end to the variety of things a man might make. If you think back over your life, you might remember a handmade hope chest, doll bed, or a dollhouse. Maybe you remember a treehouse or a birdhouse; a window box or a toy box; a toy car or a soapbox car; or a room or even a whole house!

On the farms that many of our parents grew up on, clothes were not the only things made out of necessity. Houses and barns were built, baskets for corn and cotton were woven, a hen house and a fence for the garden were constructed. Handmade benches held large families around the dining table. Once my father explained to me how small wagons were made by hand. After work, big hands might craft a cradle for a new baby, put together a toy wagon for Christmas, make a musical instrument, or just whittle. The need to create tools for life helped hone the skills men then used for the mere pleasure of creating. And these skills often led them to combine necessity and beauty.

FIRST PRACTICAL — THEN PRETTY

When we think of heirlooms, we usually think of something pretty, but one of my special treasures from the past started out as a wooden dynamite box. My father needed a box to store and carry his colored chalk for drawings. So he took an old dynamite box, fixed it so it opened with a hinged lid and fitted the inside with metal trays that swung out on hinges for accessibility. An old belt provided a leather strap for a handle.

When I started taking watercolor classes in college, that dynamite box became mine. My daddy painted it white, and I glued paper daisies on it, and my daddy lettered Sandy on it. Was I embarrassed to go to class with an old wooden box instead of something new? Absolutely not! I looked at the other students little fishing tackle boxes and felt that I was the only one with the real thing—an artist's paint kit. I could even sit on it if we painted outdoors! That box was made for "use," not for "pretty" or just to keep. And that box illustrates how big hands create things for use, but the combined creativity and skill of those hands endear those creations to us. They fit our needs better than anything store-bought and connect us to those hands that so often show love by meeting needs in practical ways.

"THEY NEEDED TO BE MADE"

One Christmas, when we were both little, my sister and I each received a handmade gift from Daddy. Hers was a pink doll cradle, and mine was a white doll crib with a little pink and blue lamb decal. I don't remember how old I was, I don't even remember unwrapping it, but I've never forgotten which one was made for *me*. It is a treasure now, even though it seems smaller than it did when I first opened it!

I recently asked my father why he made that cradle and bed for us. I thought he might say that we couldn't afford store-bought doll furniture, but he didn't. He simply said, "They needed to be made." A father's attentive heart knew that his little girl's "baby" doll needed a bed just like a mother knew that her little girl's "baby" needed a new dress.

A CRIB FOR THE BABY

A daddy also knows that real babies need beds, too! When my husband Rick and I were expecting our first child, the beautiful baby beds we saw in the store with their ruffled canopies were out of our financial reach. So Rick decided to build a baby bed. If you're thinking how smart I was to marry a furniture craftsman, I have to tell you that Rick had never made a stick of furniture in his life!

Rick measured the beds we saw in stores, and I drew a design that included a canopy. A friend let Rick use tools we didn't have, and we were able to buy hardware that enabled the siderail to go up and down. Building the curved canopy presented a problem, though. Rick solved that problem by soaking the wood in a neighbor's swimming pool and then bending it into a form to hold the shape until it dried.

As he worked on this beautiful oak bed, I appliquéd little animals from Noah's ark onto pastel gingham and calico quilt squares and made them into a valance for the windows, and of course I made a canopy with an eyelet lace ruffle. When his little room was perfect, our son arrived and came home to the place that, together, his parents had prepared for him with their hands and hearts. What a happy day it was!

OUR FIRST CHILD'S FIRST BED

But our little newborn outgrew that crib, and a little brother was on the way who would need it. This time Rick planned for his firstborn a single oak bed in an antique design. Two-year-old Samuel watched as his daddy cut out and prepared the parts, and Samuel started to work alongside his daddy.

One day I looked out of the kitchen and saw Samuel working by himself. He had gotten the little electric sander, turned it on, and was sanding a board! I looked at him—blue overalls, curly blond hair, and dimples—and saw that he was singing. Even though he wasn't two and a half, he had discovered the satisfaction of working with his hands!

Before the bed was finished, I found Samuel working on it again! This time he was sawing on top of the footboard with a hacksaw! I didn't punish him because I knew that he thought he was helping—but those marks just wouldn't sand out.

When the bed was finally finished (two days before the new baby arrived), it was truly beautiful. But the most precious thing to me is the saw marks it still has—those little grooves a two year old made imitating his dad and learning to work with his hands.

THE ULTIMATE HEIRLOOM

We are now living in what is, to me, the ultimate family heirloom from big, loving hands. Rick built our home from the ground up—his first whole house. I drew the plans for our Victorian home on graph paper and planned places for the old stained glass windows we had collected, an antique oak mantel, and, of course, gingerbread. Rick built our home just the way I drew it—complete with a turret!

Every square foot was built to meet our needs and our dreams. By the time we moved in, the whole family was so intimately acquainted with the structure that it didn't seem like a new place to us. We all know what's behind the walls and under the floors. We all helped pour the concrete footings under the foundation. Our younger son Jeremy helped mix mortar for the mason. Our son Samuel helped build the house with his young hands. When he was five years old, he had taken some boards, a hammer, and some nails and built a little fence connected to our smaller home. He had called me to see the new "room" he had so proudly added for me. On his sixteenth birthday, he was forty feet off the ground on the roof of our new house, actually building with hands that had become skilled from working with his dad. And what did I do besides design all this work? I provided barbecue and soft drinks and hung wallpaper (my only specialty!). The result is a work in progress that reflects our family—what we like, what we value, and what we can do with our hands.

AT THE HEART OF HOME IMPROVEMENT

Today most people don't need to handcraft a tool or piece of furniture or build a whole house or barn themselves. But they find satisfaction in improving their property and their lives in their spare time. Maybe that's the reason that do-it-yourself home improvement is so popular now. These do-it-yourselfers are also reflecting themselves in their work—what they like, what they value, and what they can do with their hands. And I'm sure many of these grownups sing while they work with their hands—just like my contented two year old.

Let me offer four tips for encouraging creativity in your home.

· Assume that the project will not be finished on time. You'll be more patient that way!

· Learn to tolerate a mess. It's a sign of progress.

· Remember that every craftsman needs an appreciative audience. Applaud each bit of progress you see!

· Understand that there really is a tool for every job—and it usually must be purchased.

Just as the need for creativity is frequently pulled through generations by a needle, it can also be woven through generations with nails. Rough hands show love the same way soft hands do—by meeting needs and in the process they satisfy the need to create.

Creative Little Hands

Do you remember the satisfaction of a well turned-out mud pie? I certainly do. When I was a little girl, making good mud pies was an art that required skill. It was important to use "clean" dirt (rocks or twigs could spoil a smooth surface), and mixing the right amount of water in the dirt was important to the drying time. As we played under a shade tree in our outdoor "kitchen," we made our mud pies in little aluminum muffin tins. Some were actually the mixing pans we used for paint at school. One pan we had turned out fluted pies like little Bundt cakes. To create a flawless one was a triumph! Making mud pies required both patience and diligence. It took time for the pies to dry—but not too much time. If you forgot them, they got too hard and difficult to turn out. I'll never forget the satisfaction I felt when I turned out a good mud pie. I remember how smooth it felt to my small fingers and how proud and happy I was that it hadn't broken or crumbled.

Even a child can have a vision for his creative efforts. Whether he's building a fort in the backyard or she's striving to make the perfect mud pie for her tea party, children can show real determination to finish the project they start, to persist until it's just right, and to celebrate their vision-become-reality. If you are low on inspiration or enthusiasm, let a child lead you!

If you have a child, is he or she doing anything that gives as much satisfaction as a well-turned out mud pie gave me? There is great value in making something with our hands, even if it's just a mud pie.

A GIFT FOR OUR CHILDREN

"Hobby" seems to be a word in danger of disappearing from our vocabulary. But a good hobby provides children an avenue of accomplishment other than music, dance, or sports. A hobby can help children explore their personal interests and develop their unique talents and abilities. Children who do not know how to do anything may depend too much on the media for entertainment, but children who have learned to be creative and how to work with their hands are never bored. A hobby can be an adventure in learning traditional skills, discovering the joy of creating, and experiencing the deep satisfaction that comes with finishing a job. A hobby is a gift we give to our children, a gift that keeps on giving pleasure.

GIVING THE GIFT

Needlework is not just for girls! Boys as well as girls can enjoy working with a needle and thread. When my sister and I were young, we learned how to embroider things. I always loved the threads that were variegated. The way the color changed from pink to green to lilac to yellow to blue and back to pink again was—and still is—so pretty to me. It was fun to iron on a design and embroider dresser scarves or tea towels to entertain ourselves. Elementary school children can also learn to embroider or may even do counted cross stitch. Boys or girls may have fun lacing leather crafts or learning to sew beads Indian style onto a shirt or a fringed pouch. Children can also have a wonderful time learning to use a needle and thread by making costumes from scraps of fabric. While they're having fun, they may be developing mending skills they will need as college students.

It has been fascinating for me to watch the seasons of creativity in my son Jeremy's life and the variety of projects—needlework and otherwise—that interest him. When he was four, he enjoyed taping pieces of paper together into a fireman's uniform and equipment. In elementary school, he not only drew pictures with crayons and painted paintings of ships and sharks, but he also built model boats out of balsa wood and foam core. He regularly wanted me to purchase camouflage cloth so he could make accessories for his play adventures. He was very resourceful in creating costumes and making what he didn't have from what he had on hand. To Jeremy, an empty jelly container at a restaurant was not trash; it was simply a boat that needed a sail. With a little customizing, an adult eyeglass case was a holster for his toy gun. When he got interested in fishing, it was inevitable that he would tie his own flies for trout. If he was sitting down, his hands were usually busy with a project. Does he want to be an artist or a craftsman? No, he wants to be a district attorney. But one of the things he misses most when he's away at college is working with his hands. When he has free time at home, I can hear him in the basement, sawing, grinding, and sanding late into the night. And I know that he is content.

If you would like to encourage creativity but you don't know where to begin, take your children to a craft store or fabric store. Browse with them and see what they're drawn to. You're likely to find instructions and supplies you need for a variety of projects right there. Classes or kits may also be available. And grandparents usually have many creative skills they're delighted to teach.

For your children to be creative at home, you will probably have to allow some messes. (Note that I said "messes," not "damage." A mess is something that can be cleaned up!) Learning to clean up is also a worthwhile skill for a child to learn! A creative hobby can help produce:

A contented child who is comfortable working independently.

A productive child who has things he wants to do.

A self-confident child who knows she can do something and do it well.

A child who carries on the tradition of heirlooms made by creative hands.

An extra benefit is that creative children love to be home because there is so much for them to do.

An Heirloom from Little Hands

Stop reading for just a minute. Go into your kitchen and open the drawer next to your stove and look for an heirloom made by little hands. What are you looking for? You are looking for a woven potholder. Do you remember making one? Do you remember how proud you were when you presented it to your mother? You may say, "A potholder? An heirloom?" Of course it is! It is an heirloom from little hands because no child ever made a potholder for himself. Every one was made for Mama.

Do you remember making a potholder on those square metal looms with the teeth all the way around them? Do you remember the loops of knit fabric that came in a big bag? You first had to decide whether to use one color, or two colors for a checkerboard, or more colors for a rainbow effect. Then, hoping no one had taken all the reds, you would dig through the pack of loops to find just the colors you wanted. The weaving was fun, but it was a little difficult to finish off all the loops and keep the potholder from unraveling. Near the end, all the loops started coming off the loom at the same time, so you had to kind of hold them on to the loom as you did the finishing so your weaving wouldn't come undone.

Do you remember how proud you were then as you presented your finished potholder to your mama?

My Dear Mother,
Yesterday I sent you a little Christmas box. I am very sorry that I could not send it before...but I could not finish the watch-case any sooner.
I made all of the gifts...I hope you will like your watch-case, for it made me very happy to make it for you.

HELEN KELLER

OTHER KEEPSAKES FROM LITTLE HANDS

Potholders probably aren't the only heirlooms from little hands you'll find at your house. Your child may have pressed a little hand into plaster at school. The teacher stuck a paper clip in the top before the plaster set so you could hang it up. And when it was dry, the teacher let your son paint his little handprint, the hand in white and perhaps the background in a pastel color. I made a handprint in first grade that I still have, and I also have one my child made. At the time, my hand swallowed up that little hand when we crossed the street, but now it's bigger than mine. That plaster handprint is truly an heirloom made by little hands that will never be that size again. Maybe your keepsake from little hands is a valentine made from red construction paper and heart-shaped paper doilies with stickers stuck on it and, in delightfully crooked writing that says, "Happy Valentine's Day to Mom." Or maybe you have a paper plate with yarn woven around the edge and tied in a bow with a crayon drawing in the middle. Each of these precious heirlooms from little hands was made with the anticipation of pleasing Mama. So, when that little one comes to you with, "Look what I made," label each item with the name of the child and the date (you think you'll remember, but you might not) and put them in a safe place. Treasure that gift for what it is—an heirloom from little hands.

A CHILD'S JOY

When a child gives you a trivet made of Popsicle sticks, a leather coin purse she laced together, or a tempera painting he did at school, look at the glow on that precious face and see in it the joy that was had creating the gift. Encourage your little ones to create things for the mere joy of creating, and save every creation you can. But if your child is so creative that he makes more things than you could ever keep or bulky things that you have no place to store, make these into heirlooms by taking a photograph of your child holding the special creation and date it. Make an album of all that creativity. When your children are older, you will be able to look back together and see all the wonderful things they made. And, hopefully, creating for the pure joy of creating will become your real family heirloom.

Heirlooms for Little Hands

When a precious new life begins, both friends and family want to record that event for the future. Although the baby will have no personal memory of the excitement his or her arrival will bring, we often mark the arrival of a new little one into the world with handmade keepsakes and personalized gifts. These are indeed a wonderful way to celebrate the blessed event. They testify in a tangible way to the value of this new life, and the discovery of these special things later can show an older child how much people have loved him or her from the beginning. These kinds of keepsakes are equally important for an adopted child. They are symbols of immediate love and acceptance into the family. These handmade gifts embrace the whole family, saying, "Because I love you, I already love this little one I don't yet know."

HANDMADE FOR BABY

At a wonderful baby shower for our firstborn, every guest received a square of cloth. During the party, each woman embroidered her name on her square. These fabric squares were given to me to be made into a baby quilt. (I made that little quilt, but if the expectant mother doesn't sew, someone else could put it together for her.) Shortly after our baby was born, we moved three thousand miles away. What a comfort it was to lay him on that quilt of familiar names! It is indeed a keepsake for me, still reminding me of the kindness and generosity of those dear friends and prompting me to show that kindness to others.

A handmade gift need not be complicated to make to become a treasure. One family made our son a simple blue seersucker baby blanket with his full name and birth date embroidered on it. When he is older and finds this blanket, I hope he will be blessed to realize that a family that did not yet know him took time to note his birth. Their gift made us feel so loved and special that, soon afterwards, I made one myself and mailed it to a college friend to celebrate the birth of her first child.

My tendency to stitch something special to celebrate an event is instinctive. In between diaper changes and feedings after my first child was born, I was compelled to record those statistics that only new parents care about. I appliquéd and embroidered a Noah's ark wall hanging with animals exuberantly waving signs that said "7 lbs. 13 oz." and "2:05 A.M." When my second child was born, I made a wall hanging proclaiming his vital statistics. As children, my boys never seemed particularly impressed by my sacrifice of time, but one day as adults, when they rediscover those wall-hangings, I hope they will just beam at the realization that their arrival brought great joy.

A GIFT OF LOVE FOR A NEW BABY

Choose a soft, lightweight fabric like seersucker or flannel. Cut two squares thirty-six inches wide. Embroider the name and birth date of the new wee one on one piece of fabric on the right side. Use the other piece as a backing to cover the back of the embroidery.

Put the right sides of both pieces together and stitch a little lace in the seam. Leave a small gap in the seam so that you can turn it right side out. Then stitch the gap you left with a needle and thread. (Experienced sewers: put right sides together, stitch, and turn.)

IDEAS FOR BABIES

· *Several friends took the time to crochet afghans for our firstborn. Each one was unique, and I treasure each one. As they kept Samuel snug and warm, I couldn't help but think of the thoughtfulness that produced those afghans. As Samuel has grown up, he has gotten to know each friend whose busy hands helped keep him warm when he was young.*

· *Crocheted booties are a classic handmade baby gift. If you've never crocheted, ask an older woman to teach you. You just may end up with a charming skill and a new friend. My friend Lyn learned smocking that very way.*

· *A hand-smocked baby dress or boy's jumper would be treasured by any mother. When I was expecting, my mother made a little blue baby dress that I still have. It is precious to me because it was made with a grandmothers love and anticipation.*

· *The classic keepsake baby dress is the christening dress with it's lace and tucks. If you know how to sew and could make one for a special newborn, I know it would always be treasured.*

· *I'm always touched by the little handmade baby bonnets I see in antique stores. Someone took time to make something timeless!*

· *A touch of embroidery can also make a baby gift special. You might enjoy cross-stitching a bib or embroidering a birth announcement for a nursery pillow or wall hanging.*

The joy of a new birth expressed in the joy of creating a keepsake—what a beautiful tradition for a blessed event!

FAMILY TRADITIONS, FAMILY FUN

What family traditions have you inherited? Which ones have you developed? Traditions—whether passed down through several generations or new with your own—are intangible heirlooms which greatly enrich our life today. Like tangible heirlooms, traditions can be simple or elaborate. Consider some of the following:

· *Choose a special spot in your home to display a collection of family photographs in a variety of frames. Change the photos to mark important family events. In Jeremy's birthday month, we celebrate him with pictures through the years. When it's Samuel's birthday, it's his turn to be in the spotlight.*

· *Easter-egg dying is another creative tradition at our house. On the Saturday before Easter, we gather up eight or ten teacups or mugs and three dozen boiled eggs and head outside. We line the cups up on a picnic table, porch, or board and partially fill the cups with water. The boys then mix their own colors straight from bottles of food coloring. They move the eggs from cup to cup with their hands until they get the exact and often unique color they want. We always take a picture of their green and brown and blue hands! (Bleach cleans up their hands and clothes.) After 20 years of innovations, last year we produced some lovely marbled eggs and even a black one!*

· *When I was a young girl, we had a very sweet Mother's Day tradition. On Mother's Day, we each picked a rose to wear to church. One rose for my daddy made a simple boutonniere, but my mother, my sister, and I liked ours to be more like corsages. When we had saved the pipe cleaner and ruffled net form from an old corsage, we could add our rose to that or we could simply tie it with a pretty ribbon. It was a time-honored custom to wear a red rose if your mother was living and a white one if she had passed on. It was always a sweet sight to see all the roses at church and to take note of the colors friends wore. My family honors me with a corsage for Mother's Day now, and my husband makes sure it is red to honor my mother as well and to carry on this lovely tradition.*

· *Our Christmas mornings begin with a fire in the fireplace, built by my early-rising husband. Before we enjoy the surprises under the tree, Rick reads the Christmas story from his Bible, and afterwards I serve juice and sweet rolls for a quick Christmas breakfast around the tree. Rick usually has a surprise wrapped for me under the tree or in my stocking. But it's not a gift—it's a clue. If I can decipher the clue, it will lead me—not to my gift—but to the second clue. He leads me on a merry chase until I find my gift at last. One year I looked in a neighbor's trash can, and I had to knock on another neighbor's door and ask them if they had my gift (they didn't). I finally found it by entering the home of a friend who was out of town. The effort was worth-while, though. I still cherish my antique oak secretary.*

· *One Christmas when we were dating, Rick began a very special tradition in our family by giving me a gold signet with an "L" for my maiden name. Unfortunately, I lost the ring, and he teased me unmercifully about losing it. On our wedding day, however, he replaced the ring with a new signet ring with my new monogram, a "C." In a few years, I gave Rick a gold signet ring for a gift. As each of our boys reached the age of 13, we had a milestone celebration. We invited family friends to a dinner and asked them to read special blessings they had composed to our son as he embarked on his teenage years and young adulthood. We wanted a special symbol to give to our boys to mark this important time when they were growing from boys into men, and we chose a signet ring. Each son received a gold signet ring with his monogram as a keepsake. Our oldest son Samuel was married this year, and as we anticipated adding a new member to our family for the first time in twenty-one years, we knew what we would give her as a symbol of our love and acceptance—a gold signet ring. At the rehearsal dinner before the wedding, we presented our lovely daughter-in-law Deana with a signet ring as a keepsake of becoming a Clough and changing her monogram from an "L" to a "C."*

The heart is like a treasure chest that's
filled with souvenirs. It's there we keep the
memories we gather through the years.

AUTHOR UNKNOWN

Christmas Heirlooms

Heirlooms connect us to important events and people in the past. At Christmastime, our decorations—accumulated through the years—tell stories of Christmases gone by, of people we celebrated with, of gifts given, of love shared.

And, like me, you may have noticed at your house how every Christmas includes parts of every other Christmas you've celebrated. Christmas is the most important holiday of the year for many families, and the memories and the decorations are cumulative. Christmas heirlooms add a fresh warmth to our lives because they're not like keepsakes that are boxed up and stored for years, nor are they treasures that we take for granted because we use them every day. Christmas memories are unpacked on schedule every year, and because we haven't seen or thought about them during the year, the heirlooms delight us by being both old and new.

OUR FIRST CHRISTMAS

Our family Christmas decorations go all the way back to Year One of our marriage when my husband Rick was studying for his master's degree and I was working as a teacher's aide. Our funds were very limited, and our efficiency apartment was so efficient that the living room and the bedroom were the same! For our first Christmas, we were given permission to cut down a free cedar tree in the country. When we unfolded our sofa into a bed, the Christmas tree hung over part of the mattress.

We were able to budget $3.00 each to buy Christmas presents for each other, but we couldn't afford much for Christmas decorations, so I made our ornaments.

I bought squares of colored felt and cut out angels, bells, and Christmas toys. I held two of each shape together, put a little stuffing in the middle, and stitched the edges together with a needle and some embroidery thread. I cut out details from scraps of felt and glued them on. Rick and I also made stockings for each other out of red felt and personalized them with our names and little felt cut-outs that reflected our own interests. Those little ornaments were so simple, but when I see them every Christmas, I can still remember the joy I had making them.

HISTORY IN A BOX

As I unpack the Christmas boxes every year, I find not only those first ornaments but also the dough-art ornaments I made with a friend. And every year I hang the lovely bejeweled balls sent to us one year by a neighbor I hardly knew. We had befriended her teenage son, and I knew this expression of thanks had cost her not only many hours of pushing pins into Styrofoam balls to secure the pearls, sequins, and bits of jewelry and ribbon but also some sore fingers. Every year when I unpack those sparkling ornaments, I enjoy her thoughtfulness all over again.

As our children moved through elementary school and Sunday school, they brought home special ornaments for our tree. There is a Nativity scene made from a cardboard box, a candy cane made of red and white beads threaded on wire, and a snowman made out of cotton balls. Along with these, I find other ornaments made by special people. There are cross-stitched designs in little frames and a white crocheted dove sent to us from Africa. Every handmade ornament or decoration is a keepsake because it was made just for our family. Whoever made it joyfully created it to show their love, and their effort delights us.

When I unpack these treasures, our family history unfolds before me, and I know that when I pack it up after the first of the New Year we will have added to that history and our collection of memories.

MAKING A MEMORY TREE

If you cherish all the decorations made by little hands, friendly hands, and family hands, but you want a special theme or particular look for your Christmas tree, consider having a second tree and using these keepsakes to make it a memory tree. One Christmas I put a tree on our upstairs landing and decorated it with old ornaments and handmade ornaments that didn't seem to fit on our tree anymore. I also placed old toys from past Christmases—from my childhood and my children's—under the tree. It was charming!

My friend Carolyn made a memory tree using clear plastic ornaments she found at a craft sore. Round or shaped like a heart or a bell, these hinged ornaments open and close and are usually filled with potpourri and hung. But Carolyn filled these ornaments with family memorabilia. One held a tiny pair of baby shoes, and a small nosegay and a ribbon decorated the top. Carolyn's tree was a very sweet way to display and enjoy the things we usually keep packed away.

Sandy Lynam Clough

KEEPSAKE STOCKINGS

Christmas stockings easily become keepsakes when we use the same ones every year, and a stocking made by loving hands grows especially dear with age.

· Make a stocking out of red fabric or bits of favorite old fabrics pieced together like a quilt.

· Use old quilts or favorite jeans for a stocking that has real character.

· Stockings can be made of velvet with beautiful trims or crafted from needlepoint or counted cross-stitch.

· Start with an already-made stocking and personalize it. Embroider on it, use fabric paint, or cut out letters from felt and glue them on.

Time will make your stocking—made with love and whatever else—a keepsake.

HANDMADE BY KIDS

The Christmas season offers wonderful opportunities for you to give your children many happy hours making simple Christmas decorations—and even gifts—that celebrate the season.

· *With some strips of Christmas wrapping paper or colored construction paper and some glue or a stapler, you can make paper chains.*

· *Roll pine cones first in glue and then in glitter and hang them on the tree or group them around candles with greenery.*

· *Use Styrofoam balls as the base for snowmen or decorate them with sequins, beads, and ribbons for an elegant touch.*

· *The ideas go on and on. If you don't know where to start, visit a craft store for ideas and instructions. Don't be afraid to try anything that looks interesting. After all, providing your children with an opportunity to experience the joy of creating—at Christmas and throughout the year—is more important than producing a masterpiece. And I know you'll find great joy in making Christmas decorations together and then in using them year after year to deck your halls.*

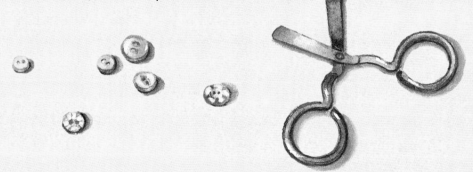

TWO LITTLE RED STOCKINGS

While going through our Christmas things this year, I found a plain little red Christmas stocking that I had forgotten about. I had made that little stocking out of red felt many years ago and had left it plain because it was for Anonymous. We were expecting our first baby close to Christmas that year, but we didn't know what to put on the stocking. Would we need a stocking for Laura or Samuel? Were we having a boy or a girl? Would our baby have brown eyes or blue? Our new baby was a wrapped present and a mystery even to us, so the stocking remained undecorated. We hung up this plain red stocking in honor of "Anonymous" and in great anticipation of meeting this mysterious new member of the family. Well, Christmas came and went, and our little stocking remained "Anonymous" because Samuel decided to be the first baby of the new year and front-page news. That simple little home-made stocking made by such expectant hands had been stored away and forgotten. We were—and still are—too busy discovering what a wonderful gift our little Anonymous was!

I found another little stocking in that box, but it wasn't mine. I never had a Christmas stocking as a child. We just hung up my daddy's socks because he had the biggest feet in the family. This little red stocking belongs to my husband Rick, and one of his mother's friends made stockings for each child in his family when he was still "Ricky." She sewed it out of red cotton and added a cuff of white flannel on the top. On the cuff, she neatly embroidered "Ricky" and sewed a little bell on the toe. When my mother-in-law's little boy grew up and left home, she sent him his special stocking. This sweet little stocking was never big enough to hold many toys or goodies, but now it holds years of Christmas memories.

CHRISTMAS CRAFTS

With a needle and thread, you can add many different items to your family's Christmas traditions. Tree skirts, tablecloths, pillows and wall-hangings as well as stockings are showcases for your creativity and care whether you choose to quilt (using pieces of Christmas fabric), needlepoint, or do counted cross-stitch, embroidery, or crewelwork. You might even knit the Christmas stockings. Use a crochet hook and white thread to create snowflakes. Starched and ironed, they are beautiful on the Christmas tree. Or, rather than using a needle and thread, consider stenciling your fabric decorations with a Christmas motif. A handmade part of your Christmas decor will become a family treasure as, year after year, it is seasoned with Christmas memories.

CHRISTMAS PICTURES

Deliberately making memories adds continuity to our lives in the midst of our rapidly changing world, and photographs mark the memories for us in such a distinctive way. You can multiply the joy of past Christmases by remembering them in photos you hang on your tree. Frame small photos in lightweight plastic frames and hang them with narrow ribbons. You might choose a theme and display annual Christmas portraits of your children or candid family photos from Christmas morning. Whatever you decide, unpacking those photographs every year will mean wonderful memories prompted by Oh, remember the year when...

Behind every joyful Christmas season are busy hands and loving hands that make the memories and then pack it all up for next year when once again they'll have the joy of unpacking the memories again. This Christmastime ritual gives continuity to the life of a family and allows for regular visits with special heirlooms from loving hands.

HEIRLOOMS FROM THE NINETIES

I recently discovered an exciting product called Quiltmakers Transfer Paper. This transfer paper allows you to copy photographs onto fabric without harming the photos in any way. After first color-copying a photo onto this transfer paper (available at quilting stores), you can iron the image on to your fabric. Consider the possibilities!

Imagine a quilt with vintage family photos on some of the squares. The squares could be held together by bands of fabric from special family clothing. A single vintage photo would make a precious keepsake pillow. Or let a sequence of photos to tell a story. Using a simple white sheet, you could make a special birthday tablecloth for each family member—adding a new birthday photo each year! Make a Christmas tablecloth using photos of past Christmases and, again, add new photos every year. Put photos of all the grandchildren on a sweatshirt or apron for Grandmother. I could go on and on! This process provides a way to combine photographs with needlework for a very personal keepsake.

An Invitation to Create

If you want to continue (or even start) linking your generation to the next with heirlooms but feel like you can't or don't have time to make anything, don't lose heart. You can do something very important that maybe your grandmother or great-grandmother could not have done. Take pictures—and take pictures often! You can find real joy in using a camera to record memories.

Photograph your child with the teacher the first day of school and the last day. Photograph every relative you can and every home you move away from. Take pictures of your pets and the year's first snowball fight. Even if you're the family photographer, don't forget to include yourself in some pictures. Put names and dates on the back of every photo. Someday they'll tell a life story and be an heirloom from your loving hands.

You can also use your camera to catalog any handmade keepsakes you have. Including in the album a story about the maker and placing it alongside the photo will help ensure that the thread of memory is not broken.

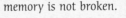

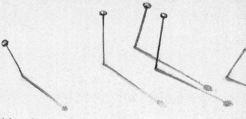

SHARING THE JOY

Whether you have family heirlooms or have adopted handmade items to cherish as your own, think for a moment about the time the crafter spent making what you treasure. . . the joy she had doing it. . . and begin to realize how that person's joy can add joy to your life. Tiny crocheted booties for a baby you'll never know. . . a sampler with countless French knots and careful satin stitching. . . a quilt of carefully planned squares. . . a tablerunner with delicate stitching in classic red thread—whatever grabs your heart and whoever made it, cherish the object as you imagine the joy that was had in its creation.

That shared joy of creating can be yours. You, too, can make heirlooms as a way of sharing your love with other people. Don't be threatened by the idea that handcrafts might be difficult. You don't need to be an accomplished artist, a polished seamstress, or a woodworker's apprentice. Almost every stitched thing and many other handcrafts as well involve basic skills that anyone can learn. Inborn talent isn't necessary, and many lovely and helpful patterns are available to guide you.

So think about using your loving hands to make an heirloom for someone else. The joy of creating that you discover—or rediscover—can give joy for years to come!

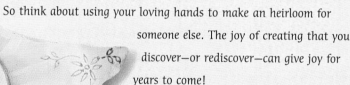

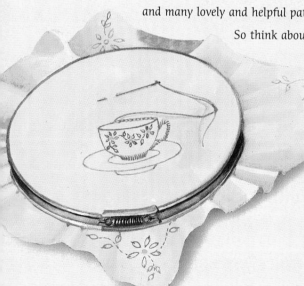

62

63

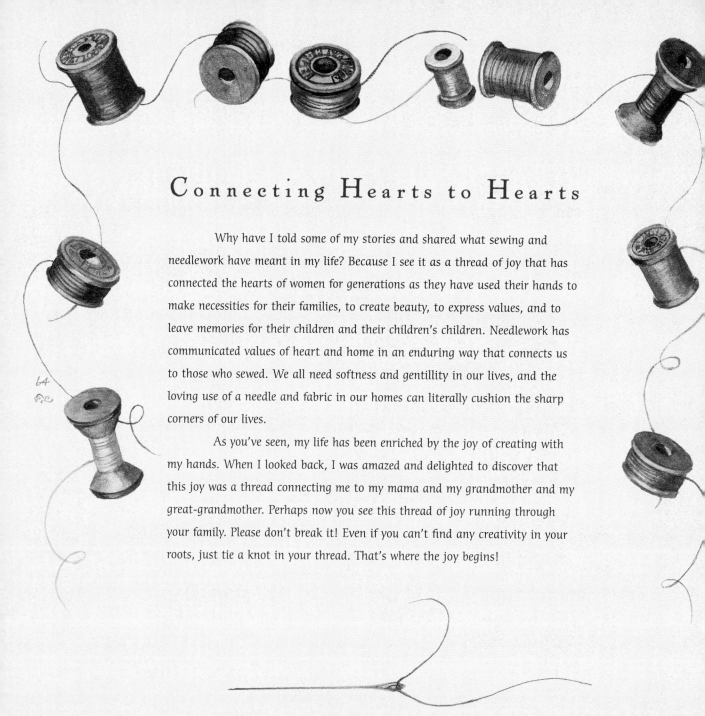

Connecting Hearts to Hearts

Why have I told some of my stories and shared what sewing and needlework have meant in my life? Because I see it as a thread of joy that has connected the hearts of women for generations as they have used their hands to make necessities for their families, to create beauty, to express values, and to leave memories for their children and their children's children. Needlework has communicated values of heart and home in an enduring way that connects us to those who sewed. We all need softness and gentillity in our lives, and the loving use of a needle and fabric in our homes can literally cushion the sharp corners of our lives.

As you've seen, my life has been enriched by the joy of creating with my hands. When I looked back, I was amazed and delighted to discover that this joy was a thread connecting me to my mama and my grandmother and my great-grandmother. Perhaps now you see this thread of joy running through your family. Please don't break it! Even if you can't find any creativity in your roots, just tie a knot in your thread. That's where the joy begins!